The Mindfulness Rx Journal

- Track your meditation time
- Review each day's lesson
- Reinforce positive traits to last a lifetime

Valerie Foster and Bill Van Ollefen

Published by Pathway to Mindfulness, www.PathwayToMindfulness.com, info@PathwayToMindfulness.com.

This is the companion book to The Mindfulness Rx: 56 Days, 56 Ways to find emotional and physical peace, which is based on the first eight weeks of mindfulness training at Pathway to Mindfulness.

*"When you journal you review
and reflect, which helps you
understand yourself better
and begin to make
positive changes for your future."*

– Pathway to Mindfulness

Introduction

Should you journal? How many ways can we say **YES!**

At Pathway to Mindfulness, we suggest to all our clients that they journal, even when they look at us with glassy eyes and cry: "I hate to journal!" We get it.

Valerie has always kept a journal, understanding that she gained so much insight into herself by writing – and then reading – her thoughts.

Bill? Well let's say he came into the practice of journaling kicking and screaming. Softly of course, because after all, we are meditation teachers. But once journaling became a habit, he began to understand how his journal really can be one of the greatest tools he has on his mindfulness journey.

How? In a nutshell: By jotting down your thoughts that came up during meditation, it gives you the chance to think about them outside meditation. Journaling also:

- Brings self-awareness and insight, and we teach insight mindfulness meditation.
- It can bring some clarity to the issues in your life that are troubling you.
- It can provide answers to something that you have been thinking about, but the solution was elusive.
- It's a safe place to write about you.
- It helps you set intentions about the parts of your life you would like to change.

This journal is a companion to our book, *The Mindfulness Rx: 56 days, 56 ways to find emotional and physical peace.*

We wish you ease and awakening as you begin your journey of a lifetime, which we hope you realize is an ongoing process, and one you practice for the rest of your life.

Kindly,

Valerie and Bill

This Journal Belongs to

_____

Before you begin to record your journey into mindfulness, take a few minutes and think about what you hope to achieve by journaling daily for the next 56 days.

_____

_____

_____

_____

_____

_____

_____

And one bit of advice!

Either journal every night before you go to bed, or first thing in the morning about the previous day. Our preference is for you to choose the nighttime, which acts as a great bridge between your day and your sleep. But choose whatever works best for you and then make a commitment, right here and right now, that you will journal daily.

I _____commit to journal daily.

Date: _____

DAY 1

***The journey of a thousand miles begins
with a single step." – Lao Tzu***

Today, you were asked to do three things.

1. Did I read and sign my contract? **Yes? No?**

2. What contract points are most important to me right now?

_____

_____

_____

_____

_____

3. How do I honestly feel about journaling?

_____

_____

_____

_____

4. Today, right now, will I consider the possibility that journaling can truly help me understand myself? **Yes? No?**

5. Did I give someone I love or admire an unexpected hug? **Yes? No?**

6. If yes, how did that make me feel?

_____

_____

_____

7. Did I take five deep breaths, slowly and quietly? Did I feel the breath as it entered my nose, traveling down to my tummy, and follow the exhale as it left my body, either through my nose or mouth? **Yes? No?**

8. How did the deep breaths make me feel?

_____

_____

_____

_____

9. My mindful thoughts for the day:

_____

_____

_____

_____

_____

_____

_____

_____

_____

_____

_____

_____

_____

_____

_____

_____

_____

_____

_____

DAY 2

*"Do you look at your day as happy and colorful
or gloomy and gray? It all comes down
to the box of crayons you choose to color
your world. This choice is up to you, no matter what life
throws your way." – Pathway to Mindfulness*

Today you learned about the meditation style we teach – centuries' old vipassana meditation, which translates as insight mindfulness meditation. It is a gentle practice that builds awareness and can be practiced anywhere, because all you need is yourself. It is unguided, which is why we are starting your meditation journey very slowly.

Science tells us that meditating 20 minutes most days is what changes our brains and patterns of behavior. We promise that if you believe and do the work, you will reach that 20 minutes by the end of these 56 days – if not weeks before.

1. Today I was asked to pay attention to brushing my teeth: First, running my tongue over my teeth; as I flossed, identifying the teeth that are closer together, the ones that are farther apart; the taste of my toothpaste; the sensation of my water flosser and mouthwash; and finally, running my tongue back over my teeth to feel if there is a difference. Did I do this exercise? **Yes? No?**

2. How did this exercise make me feel?

_____

_____

_____

3. Was there a difference between the way my teeth felt before the brushing and after?

_____

_____

_____

4. Today I was asked to sit quietly for two minutes, simply breathing as I did yesterday, eyes open or closed. Did I breathe slowly, calmly and quietly? **Yes? No?**

5. Did I focus on my breath as I inhaled and exhaled? **Yes? No?**

6. How did this exercise make me feel?

_____

_____

_____

7. My mindful thoughts for the day:

_____

_____

_____

_____

_____

_____

_____

_____

_____

_____

_____

_____

_____

_____

DAY 3

"When you arise in the morning, think of what a precious privilege it is to be alive – to breathe, to think, to enjoy, to love." – Marcus Aurelius

Today you learned about three anchors to use during meditation. Thoughts will always arise during meditation; the anchor is there to gently break your thought pattern and allow you to return to your breath.

1. Did I meditate for one minute, using the first anchor – focusing attention on my breathing? **Yes? No?**

2. Will I use this anchor in my daily meditation? **Yes? No?**

3. Did I meditate for one minute, using the second anchor – visualizing something that brings me peace? **Yes? No?**

4. Will I use this anchor in my daily meditation? **Yes? No?**

5. Did I meditate for one minute, using the third anchor – counting? **Yes? No?**

6. Will I use this anchor in my daily meditation? **Yes? No?**

7. Did I walk around my home, looking at the pictures on my walls with a fresh eye, as if looking at them for the first time? **Yes? No?**

8. Any surprises pop up while I was looking?

_____

_____

_____

_____

9. Did I practice any of the anchors throughout the day? **Yes? No?**

10. How do I feel about the anchors?

_____

_____

_____

11. My mindful thoughts for the day:

_____

_____

_____

_____

_____

_____

_____

_____

_____

_____

_____

_____

_____

_____

_____

_____

_____

_____

_____

_____

DAY 4

"When we practice loving kindness and compassion, we are the first ones to profit." – Rumi

Today we emphasized the importance of loving kindness and self-compassion because both are often ignored. Our philosophy: The more you love yourself the more you can show love to someone else.

1. What happens if I always put everyone else first?

_____

_____

_____

2. How do I define self-care?

_____

_____

_____

_____

3. Is it important for me to judge myself less? **Yes? No?**

4. How would life change if I judged myself less?

_____

_____

_____

_____

5. Is it important for me to judge others less? **Yes? No?**

6. How would life be if I judged others less?

_____

_____

_____

7. What did I think of the Mindfulness Awareness Survey?

_____

_____

_____

8. Is there anything in this survey I would like to work on?

_____

_____

_____

9. Did I meditate for three minutes today? **Yes? No?** What thoughts came up?

_____

_____

_____

10. Did I breathe deeply and quietly? **Yes? No?**

11. When thoughts came up did I notice them, make no judgment, and return to my breath using an anchor? **Yes? No?**

12. What anchor(s) did I use?_____

13. How did the experience go?

_____

_____

_____

14. My mindful thoughts for the day:

_____

_____

_____

_____

DAY 5

*"Meditation is an exercise of the mind,
so practice in any position that makes
you comfortable." – Pathway to Mindfulness*

Today we talked about meditation postures and explained that we view meditation as an exercise of the mind and not the body. No matter your position – on a chair, standing, sitting cross-legged on a meditation cushion, or lying down – you will benefit the same from the practice.

The how you meditate is just not that important to us, and this is what we teach our clients.

1. Did I meditate while sitting on a chair? **Yes? No?**

2. Is this comfortable for me? **Yes? No?**

3. Was I able to sit up straight, but not overly tight, opening my chest, which allows my breath to travel through my body? **Yes? No?**

4. Did I close my eyes? **Yes? No?**

5. Cast my eyes down? **Yes? No?**

6. Or soften my gaze, not fixed on anything? **Yes? No?**

7. Did I relax my body where tension accumulates most: shoulders, neck, jaw, eyes, mouth? **Yes? No?**

8. Did I begin the twice-a-day ritual of saying the words: "I love you (my name)?" **Yes? No?**

9. Was I able to say these words to my current self? **Yes? No?**

10. If I imagined my younger self, how old was I? _____

11. Did I log onto www.PathwayToMindfulness.com to listen to the meditation titled semi-guided meditation? **Yes? No?**

12. Or, did I read the words in the book? **Yes? No?**

13. Did I find the meditation comforting? **Yes? No?**

14. My mindful thoughts for the day:

_____

_____

_____

_____

_____

_____

_____

_____

_____

_____

_____

_____

_____

_____

_____

_____

_____

_____

_____

_____

_____

_____

_____

DAY 6

*"You're always with yourself, so you might
as well enjoy the company."
– Diane Von Furstenberg*

Today you ate a raisin in a mindful way, really exploring each of your senses as you ate one raisin.

1. What would happen if I ate everything that passes my lips in a mindful way?

_____

_____

_____

2. What food or drink did I choose to explore mindfully?

_____

_____

_____

3. Did I enjoy mindfully eating something I love? **Yes? No?** Why?

_____

_____

_____

4. Will I consider eating mindfully going forward? **Yes? No?**

5. Did I meditate for five minutes? **Yes? No?** What thoughts came up? Were any of these thoughts recurring?

_____

_____

_____

_____

6. When my thoughts appeared, did I simply notice them with no judgment and use an anchor to return to my breath? **Yes? No?**

7. What anchor(s) did I use? _____

8. Did I take five deep breaths after I told myself twice today, "I love you (my name)?" **Yes? No?**

9. My mindful thoughts for the day:

_____

_____

_____

_____

_____

_____

_____

_____

_____

_____

_____

_____

_____

_____

_____

_____

_____

_____

_____

DAY 7

> *"Give me six hours to chop down a tree*
> *and I will spend the first four sharpening*
> *the axe." – Abraham Lincoln*

To put the Lincoln quote in context: These beginning weeks are your preparation – sharpening your axe – for a lifetime lived mindfully.

Our definition of mindfulness is living in the present, not thinking about the past or worrying about the future. It is living without judgment or criticism. It is simply being, responding to life rather than reacting.

When you mindfully engage in life you learn to breathe, explore with curiosity, nourish yourself and your loved ones, and ultimately thrive. Mindfulness frees you to enjoy life, happier, healthier and more peacefully.

1. Right now, do I believe that I will be able to live this way? **Yes? No?**

2. Honestly, does it sound too good to be true? **Yes? No?**

3. Did I re-read and re-commit to my contract? **Yes? No?** If no, please do so now.

4. Did I take five deep breaths after I told myself twice today, "I love you (my name)?" **Yes? No?**

5. Did I meditate for five minutes? **Yes? No?** What thoughts came up? Were any of these thoughts recurring?

_____

_____

_____

_____

_____

_____

6. When my thoughts appeared, did I simply notice them with no judgment and use an anchor to return to my breath? **Yes? No?**

7. What anchor(s) did I use? _____

8. My mindful thoughts for the day:

_____

_____

_____

_____

_____

_____

_____

_____

_____

_____

_____

_____

_____

_____

_____

_____

_____

_____

_____

_____

_____

_____

DAY 8

*"To be an expert means that you were once
a beginner." – Pathway to Mindfulness*

Today we made a case for journaling, and if you bought this
journal, you are probably beginning to see how critical this
daily exercise can become. As you continue to journey
through *The Mindfulness Rx,* the questions we ask here
daily will not be as tied to your daily lesson, but will become
the framework for your permanent journal, the one we hope
you will keep forever.

1. Did I choose a pen or pencil to keep this journal?

_____

2. If pen, am I using different colored inks? **Yes? No?**

3. If yes, what colors did I choose and why?

_____

_____

_____

4. Do I like to journal? **Yes? No?** If yes, why?

_____

_____

6. If no, why?

_____

_____

7. Think about the good that can happen when I journal.

_____

_____

_____

_____

8. Was I able to pause and breathe deeply at least four times throughout the day? **Yes? No?**

9. How did this make me feel?

_____

_____

_____

10. Did I meditate for six minutes? **Yes? No?** What thoughts came up? Were any of these thoughts recurring?

_____

_____

_____

11. When thoughts appeared, did I notice them with no judgment and use an anchor to return to my breath? **Yes? No?**

12. What anchor(s) did I use? _____

13. Did I feel any tense spots? The meditation on Day 5 suggested that I send my breath to any part of my body that is tense, in pain or has fallen asleep. Did I do this? **Yes? No?**

14. Did I take five deep breaths after I told myself twice today, "I love you (my name)?" **Yes? No?**

15. My mindful thoughts for the day:

_____

_____

_____

_____

_____

_____

_____

DAY 9

"Meditation super charges your brain,
making you smarter, focused, more attentive,
empathetic, less reactive and well, just nicer.
How exciting is this?" – Pathway to Mindfulness

You learned today that you are never too old to change. However, it's important to keep in mind that our brains shrink as we age. Absent exercising our minds, learning and change become harder, our memories are not as sharp, critical thinking begins to dull, and we lack cognitive flexibility.

And that is why we meditate. It just keeps us more aware, engaged in life, calmer and happier.

1. Did I splash cold water on my face? **Yes? No?**

2. Did it feel good? **Yes? No?**

3. Would I like the water a little warmer? **Yes? No?**

4. Did this wake me up? **Yes? No?**

5. Is this something I would like to incorporate into my morning routine? **Yes? No?**

6. Did I meditate for seven minutes? **Yes? No?** What thoughts came up? Were any of these thoughts recurring?

_____

_____

_____

7. When my thoughts appeared, did I simply notice them with no judgment and use an anchor to return to my breath? **Yes? No?**

8. What anchor(s) did I use? _____

9. Did I feel any tense spots in my body? The meditation I did on Day 5 suggested that I send my breath to any part of my body that is tense, in pain or has fallen asleep. Did I do this? **Yes? No?**

10. Did I take five deep breaths after I told myself twice to-day, "I love you (my name)?" **Yes? No?**

11. My mindful thoughts for the day:

_____

_____

_____

_____

_____

_____

_____

_____

_____

_____

_____

_____

_____

_____

_____

_____

_____

_____

_____

_____

_____

_____

_____

DAY 10

> *"Meditation strengthens virtually every part*
> *of your brain and its functions are enhanced."*
> *– Pathway to Mindfulness*

Today you learned about how meditation changes many parts of your brain, using the hand puppet illustration to depict your brain.

1. What parts of my brain do I hope meditation strengthens the most?

_____

_____

_____

2. I learned that some anxiety is good, bringing on a burst of energy. Did I embrace my anxiety and use it to do something healthy for myself – take a walk, clean my house, organize a closet, clean my desk, go to the gym? **Yes? No?**

3. Did I meditate for eight minutes? **Yes? No?** What thoughts came up? Were any of these thoughts recurring?

_____

_____

_____

4. When my thoughts appeared, did I simply notice them with no judgment and use an anchor to return to my breath? **Yes? No?**

5. What anchor(s) did I use? _____

6. Did I feel any tense spots in my body? The meditation I did on Day 5 suggested that I send my breath to any part of my body that is tense, in pain or has fallen asleep. Did I do this? **Yes? No?**

7. Did I take five deep breaths after I told myself twice today, "I love you (my name)?" **Yes? No?**

8. My mindful thoughts for the day:

_____

_____

_____

_____

_____

_____

_____

_____

_____

_____

_____

_____

_____

_____

_____

_____

_____

_____

_____

_____

_____

_____

_____

_____

_____

_____

DAY 11

> *"Look at stress this way: Stress won't kill you.*
> *It's your reaction to stress that may!"*
> *– Pathway to Mindfulness*

Today we talked about our fight/flight/freeze mechanism that has been with man since creation, and how our bodies today respond to stressful situations the same as our ancestors.

1. Each time a stressor came into my life, did I write it down, including the time it occurred? **Yes? No?**

2. Was there a stressor that happened more than once? **Yes? No?**

3. If yes, what was it?

_____

_____

_____

4. Did I take a break and stare out a window, looking for something I have never seen before? **Yes? No?**

5. Did I meditate for eight minutes? **Yes? No?** What thoughts came up? Were any of these thoughts recurring?

_____

_____

_____

6. When thoughts appeared, did I notice them with no judgment and use an anchor to return to my breath? **Yes? No?**

7. What anchor(s) did I use? _____

8. Did I feel any tense spots in my body? The meditation I did on Day 5 suggested that I send my breath to any part of my body that is tense, in pain or has fallen asleep. Did I do this? **Yes? No?**

9. Did I take five deep breaths after I told myself twice today, "I love you (my name)?" **Yes? No?**

10. My mindful thoughts for the day:

_____

_____

_____

_____

_____

_____

_____

_____

_____

_____

_____

_____

_____

_____

_____

_____

_____

_____

_____

_____

_____

_____

_____

_____

DAY 12

*"Your greatest weakness lies in giving up.
The most certain way to succeed is always
to try just one more time." – Thomas A. Edison*

Today you learned one of the most important mindfulness concepts, the Triangle of Self-Awareness. Simply put you, your whole self, is composed of a triangle that includes your emotions, thoughts and physical sensations. While each is distinct, they continuously impact and interact with each other.

1. Did I explore my Triangle of Self-Awareness, looking at my physical sensations, my emotions and my thoughts? **Yes? No?**

2. Did these exercises help me understand how my body, emotions and thoughts are all interwoven? **Yes? No?**

3. Did I do the SAFE meditation? **Yes? No?**

4. Did I find comfort in simply thinking the word *soften*? **Yes? No?**

5. Can I think of any time I will use SAFE to help me in a difficult situation?

_____

_____

_____

6. Did I meditate for eight minutes? **Yes? No?** What thoughts came up? Were any of these thoughts recurring?

_____

_____

_____

7. When my thoughts appeared, did I simply notice them with no judgment and use an anchor to return to my breath? **Yes? No?**

8. What anchor(s) did I use? _____

9. Did I feel any tense spots in my body? The meditation I did on Day 5 suggested that I send my breath to any part of my body that is tense, in pain or has fallen asleep. Did I do this? **Yes? No?**

10. Did I take five deep breaths after I told myself twice to-day, "I love you (my name)?" **Yes? No?**

11. My mindful thoughts for the day:

_____

_____

_____

_____

_____

_____

_____

_____

_____

_____

_____

_____

_____

_____

_____

_____

_____

_____

_____

DAY 13

*"As you start noticing the pleasant events in life, you
begin to crowd out the unpleasant."
– Pathway to Mindfulness*

Today we talked about starting to notice the pleasant events
that make us happy – or at the very least, bring a tiny smile
to our faces. We suggest this for a reason: The more you're
able to notice pleasant moments, the calmer and more
peaceful your life becomes.

1. Did I search out one pleasant event? **Yes? No?** If yes,
what was it?

_____

_____

_____

_____

2. Did I search out one unpleasant event? **Yes? No?** If yes,
what was it?

_____

_____

_____

3. When I experienced any tension or anxiety today, did I
connect with my five senses, noticing what I was seeing,
smelling, feeling, tasting, hearing? **Yes? No?**

4. Did I poll my Triangle of Self-Awareness, focusing on
thoughts, emotions, physical sensations? **Yes? No?**

5. Did I meditate for nine minutes? **Yes? No?** What
thoughts came up? Were any of these thoughts recurring?

_____

_____

_____

6. When my thoughts appeared, did I simply notice them with no judgment and use an anchor to return to my breath? **Yes? No?**

7. What anchor(s) did I use? _____

8. Did I feel any tense spots in my body? The meditation I did on Day 5 suggested that I send my breath to any part of my body that is tense, in pain or has fallen asleep. Did I do this? **Yes? No?**

9. Did I take five deep breaths after I told myself twice today, "I love you (my name)?" **Yes? No?**

10. Did I do the SAFE meditation? **Yes? No?** Did I find comfort in simply thinking the word *soften*? **Yes? No?**

11. My mindful thoughts for the day:

_____

_____

_____

_____

_____

_____

_____

_____

_____

_____

_____

_____

_____

_____

_____

DAY 14

"Be the change that you wish to see in the world."
— Mahatma Gandhi

We talked a lot about stress this week, and the two statistics we hope you keep in mind are:
1. 75 percent of us are stressed!
2. 75 percent of our preventable illnesses are caused by stress!

1. Did I re-read and re-commit to my contract? **Yes? No?**

2. Did I say something nice to a stranger today? Or, if that made me uncomfortable, did I simply smile? **Yes? No?**

3. Did I pay attention to how this simple act of kindness made my body feel – physically and emotionally? **Yes? No?**

4. And what about my thoughts? **Yes? No?**

5. Did this exercise bring out my inner critic or were my thoughts telling me how terrific I am? Jot down some thoughts:

_____

_____

_____

6. Did I meditate for nine minutes? **Yes? No?** What thoughts came up? Were any of these thoughts recurring?

_____

_____

_____

7. When my thoughts appeared, did I simply notice them with no judgment and use an anchor to return to my breath? **Yes? No?**

8. What anchor(s) did I use? _____

9. Did I feel any tense spots in my body? The meditation on Day 5 suggested I send my breath to a part of my body that is tense, in pain or has fallen asleep. Did I? **Yes? No?**

10. Did I take five deep breaths after I told myself twice today, "I love you (my name)?" **Yes? No?**

11. Did I use the Triangle of Self-Awareness during a stressful situation today, which will help me respond rather than react to life's events? **Yes? No?**

12. Did I do the SAFE meditation? **Yes? No?** Did I find comfort in simply thinking the word *soften*? **Yes? No?**

13. My mindful thoughts for the day:

_____

_____

_____

_____

_____

_____

_____

_____

_____

_____

_____

_____

_____

_____

_____

DAY 15

*"There is only one person who can make
you happy: YOU!" – Pathway to Mindfulness*

As you learned, only one in three people reported being happy in a Harris survey. Today, we began to make the case for bringing a happy attitude into your daily life.

1. Did I look around today to notice little things that brought a smile to my face? **Yes? No?**

2. Did I tell myself throughout the day: "Today is a happy day and I vow to choose to be happy?" **Yes? No?**

3. Did I write down the happy events that filled my day? **Yes? No?**

4. Did I meditate for 10 minutes? **Yes? No?** What thoughts came up? Were any of these thoughts recurring?

_____

_____

_____

5. When my thoughts appeared, did I simply notice them with no judgment and use an anchor to return to my breath? **Yes? No?**

6. What anchor(s) did I use? _____

7. Did I feel any tense spots in my body? The meditation I did on Day 5 suggested that I send my breath to any part of my body that is tense, in pain or has fallen asleep. Did I do this? **Yes? No?**

8. Did I take five deep breaths after I told myself twice today, "I love you (my name)?" **Yes? No?**

9. Did I use the Triangle of Self-Awareness during a stressful situation today, which will help me respond rather than react to life's events? **Yes? No?**

10. When I hit a rough patch today, did I say the long vowel Eeeeeeeee out loud, over and over, until I laughed? **Yes? No?**

11. Did I do the SAFE meditation? **Yes? No?** Did I find comfort in simply thinking the word *soften*? **Yes? No?**

12. My mindful thoughts for the day:

_____

_____

_____

_____

_____

_____

_____

_____

_____

_____

_____

_____

_____

_____

_____

_____

_____

_____

_____

DAY 16

*"No one can make you feel inferior
without your consent." — Eleanor Roosevelt*

1. Did I write down the answers to the questions: What do I want? What do I need? What do I have? **Yes? No?**

2. Did I think of something that made me smile during the day today, reliving the experience and polling my Triangle of Self-Awareness? **Yes? No?**

3. Did I meditate for 10 minutes? **Yes? No?** What thoughts came up? Were any of these thoughts recurring?

_____

_____

_____

_____

4. When my thoughts appeared, did I simply notice them with no judgment and use an anchor to return to my breath? **Yes? No?**

5. What anchor(s) did I use? _____

6. Did I feel any tense spots in my body? The meditation I did on Day 5 suggested that I send my breath to any part of my body that is tense, in pain or has fallen asleep. Did I do this? **Yes? No?**

7. Did I take five deep breaths after I told myself twice today, "I love you (my name)?" **Yes? No?**

8. Did I use the Triangle of Self-Awareness during a stressful situation today, which will help me respond rather than react to life's events? **Yes? No?**

9. When I hit a rough patch today, did I say the long vowel Eeeeeeeee out loud, over and over, until I started to laugh? **Yes? No?**

10. Did I look around today to notice little things that brought a smile to my face? **Yes? No?**

11. Did I tell myself throughout the day: "Today is a happy day and I vow to choose to be happy?" **Yes? No?**

12. What were five happy or pleasant events that filled my day?

a._____

b. _____

c. _____

d._____

e._____

13. How does writing about these happy events make me feel now?

_____

_____

_____

14. Did I do the SAFE meditation? **Yes? No?** Did I find comfort in simply thinking the word *soften*? **Yes? No?**

15. My mindful thoughts for the day:

_____

_____

_____

_____

_____

_____

_____

_____

DAY 17

"I have not failed. I've just found 10,000 ways that won't work." — Thomas A. Edison

1. Did I meditate for 11 minutes? **Yes? No?** What thoughts came up? Were any of these thoughts recurring?

_____

_____

_____

_____

_____

2. When my thoughts appeared, did I simply notice them with no judgment and use an anchor to return to my breath? **Yes? No?**

3. What anchor(s) did I use? _____

4. Did I feel any tense spots in my body? The meditation I did on Day 5 suggested that I send my breath to any part of my body that is tense, in pain or has fallen asleep. Did I do this? **Yes? No?**

5. Did I take five deep breaths after I told myself twice today, "I love you (my name)?" **Yes? No?**

6. Did I use the Triangle of Self-Awareness during a stressful situation today, which will help me respond rather than react to life's events? **Yes? No?**

7. When I hit a rough patch today, did I say the long vowel Eeeeeeeee out loud, over and over, until I started to laugh? **Yes? No?**

8. Did I look around today to notice little things that brought a smile to my face? **Yes? No?**

9. Did I tell myself throughout the day: "Today is a happy day and I vow to choose to be happy?" **Yes? No?**

10. What were five happy or pleasant events that filled my day?

a._____

b. _____

c. _____

d._____

e._____

11. How does writing about these happy events make me feel now?

_____

_____

_____

12. Did I do the SAFE meditation? **Yes? No?** Did I find comfort in simply thinking the word *soften*? **Yes? No?**

13. My mindful thoughts for the day:

_____

_____

_____

_____

_____

_____

_____

_____

_____

_____

_____

_____

DAY 18

> *"The breath can heal and calm.*
> *Instead of reacting, when you take a breath*
> *that pause gives you the ability to respond,*
> *bringing a sense of peace into your world."*
> *— Pathway to Mindfulness*

1. Today I learned three breaths – bellows, sequence, box. Did I try each? **Yes? No?**

2. Which breath did I like best and why?

_____

_____

_____

3. Did I breathe deeply when stopped at a traffic light or caught in traffic? **Yes? No?**

4. How did this make me feel?

_____

_____

_____

5. Did I meditate for 12 minutes? **Yes? No?** What thoughts came up? Were any of these thoughts recurring?

_____

_____

_____

6. When my thoughts appeared, did I notice them with no judgment and use an anchor to return to my breath? **Yes? No?**

7. What anchor(s) did I use? _____

8. Did I send my breath to a body part that is tense, in pain or has fallen asleep during meditation? **Yes? No?**

9. Did I take five deep breaths after I told myself twice today, "I love you (my name)?" **Yes? No?**

10. Did I use the Triangle of Self-Awareness during a stressful situation today? **Yes? No?**

11. When I hit a rough patch today, did I repeat the long vowel Eeeeeeeee out loud until I laughed? **Yes? No?**

12. Did I notice little things that made me smile? **Yes? No?**

13. Did I tell myself throughout the day: "Today is a happy day and I vow to choose to be happy?" **Yes? No?**

14. Name five happy or pleasant events that filled my day.

a._____

b. _____

c. _____

d._____

e._____

15. How does writing about happy events make me feel?

_____

_____

16. Did I do the SAFE meditation? **Yes? No?** Did I find comfort in simply thinking the word *soften*? **Yes? No?**

17. My mindful thoughts for the day:

_____

_____

_____

DAY 19

"Believe in yourself!" – Pathway to Mindfulness

Today you learned about the lessons the breath teaches us.

1. When I found myself rushing, was I able to stop, take a deep breath, and slow down? **Yes? No?**

2. Did I meditate for 12 minutes? **Yes? No?** What thoughts came up? Were any of these thoughts recurring?

_____

_____

_____

3. When my thoughts appeared, did I simply notice them with no judgment and use an anchor to return to my breath? **Yes? No?**

4. What anchor(s) did I use? _____

5. Did I feel any tense spots in my body? The meditation I did on Day 5 suggested that I send my breath to any part of my body that is tense, in pain or has fallen asleep. Did I do this? **Yes? No?**

6. Did I take five deep breaths after I told myself twice today, "I love you (my name)?" **Yes? No?**

7. Did I use the Triangle of Self-Awareness during a stressful situation today, which will help me respond rather than react to life's events? **Yes? No?**

8. When I hit a rough patch today, did I say the long vowel Eeeeeeeee out loud, over and over, until I started to laugh? **Yes? No?**

9. Did I look around today to notice little things that brought a smile to my face? **Yes? No?**

10. Did I tell myself throughout the day: "Today is a happy day and I vow to choose to be happy?" **Yes? No?**

11. What were five happy or pleasant events that filled my day?

a._____

b. _____

c. _____

d._____

e._____

12. How does writing about these happy events make me feel now?

_____

_____

_____

13. Did I practice and/or use the bellows, box and sequence breathing techniques? **Yes? No?**

14. Did I do the SAFE meditation? **Yes? No?** Did I find comfort in simply thinking the word *soften*? **Yes? No?**

15. My mindful thoughts for the day:

_____

_____

_____

_____

_____

_____

_____

_____

DAY 20

"The only person in charge of you is you."
– Pathway to Mindfulness

1. Today I learned the STOP meditation. How many times during the day did I practice STOP and what were the instances?

_____

_____

_____

2. Throughout the day, was I able to relax the muscles in my face, especially around my jaw, neck and shoulders, where tension likes to hang out? Did I pay attention to what happens in my body as I relax? **Yes? No?**

3. Did I meditate for 12 minutes? **Yes? No?** What thoughts came up? Were any of these thoughts recurring?

_____

_____

_____

_____

4. When my thoughts appeared, did I simply notice them with no judgment and use an anchor to return to my breath? **Yes? No?**

5. What anchor(s) did I use? _____

6. Did I feel any tense spots in my body? The meditation I did on Day 5 suggested that I send my breath to any part of my body that is tense, in pain or has fallen asleep. Did I do this? **Yes? No?**

7. Did I take five deep breaths after I told myself twice today, "I love you (my name)?" **Yes? No?**

8. Did I use the Triangle of Self-Awareness during a stressful situation today? **Yes? No?**

9. When I hit a rough patch today, did I repeat the long vowel Eeeeeeeee out loud until I laughed? **Yes? No?**

10. Did I look around today to notice little things that brought a smile to my face? **Yes? No?**

11. Did I tell myself throughout the day: "Today is a happy day and I vow to choose to be happy?" **Yes? No?**

12. What were five happy or pleasant events that filled my day?

a._____

b. _____

c. _____

d._____

e._____

13. How does writing about these events make me feel now?

_____

_____

_____

14. Did I practice and/or use the bellows, box and sequence breathing techniques? **Yes? No?**

15. Did I do the SAFE meditation? **Yes? No?** Did I find comfort in simply thinking the word *soften*? **Yes? No?**

16. My mindful thoughts for the day:

_____

_____

_____

_____

DAY 21

*"Positive thoughts attract positive feelings
and life experiences. Choose to live life
today with your glass half full."*
– Pathway to Mindfulness

1. Did I re-read and re-commit to my contract? **Yes? No?**

2. When I was driving, did I look at my hands to see if they were tightly gripping the steering wheel? If so, did I take a breath and relax them? **Yes? No?**

3. Did I meditate for 13 minutes? **Yes? No?** What thoughts came up? Were any of these thoughts recurring?

_____

_____

_____

_____

_____

4. When my thoughts appeared, did I simply notice them with no judgment and use an anchor to return to my breath? **Yes? No?**

5. What anchor(s) did I use? _____

6. Did I feel any tense spots in my body? The meditation I did on Day 5 suggested that I send my breath to any part of my body that is tense, in pain or has fallen asleep. Did I do this? **Yes? No?**

7. Did I take five deep breaths after I told myself twice today, "I love you (my name)?" **Yes? No?**

8. Did I use the Triangle of Self-Awareness during a stressful situation today, which will help me respond rather than react to life's events? **Yes? No?**

9. When I hit a rough patch today, did I repeat the long vowel Eeeeeeeee out loud until I laughed. **Yes? No?**

10. Did I look around today to notice little things that brought a smile to my face? **Yes? No?**

11. Did I tell myself throughout the day: "Today is a happy day and I vow to choose to be happy?" **Yes? No?**

12. Name five happy or pleasant events that filled my day.

a._____

b. _____

c. _____

d._____

e._____

13. How does writing about these events make me feel?

_____

_____

14. Did I practice and/or use the bellows, box and sequence breathing techniques? **Yes? No?**

15. Did I practice and use the STOP meditation? **Yes? No?** Did I do the SAFE meditation? **Yes? No?** Did I find comfort in simply thinking the word *soften*? **Yes? No?**

16. Throughout the day, was I able to relax the muscles in my face, especially around my jaw, neck and shoulders, where tension likes to hang out? Did I pay attention to what happens in my body as I relax? **Yes? No?**

17. My mindful thoughts for the day:

_____

_____

_____

_____

DAY 22

"Yes, I can! I can do anything I put my mind to!"
– Pathway to Mindfulness

We started discussing effective communication today, which is so necessary in every aspect of our lives. You learned about basic personality traits – and tried to picture where you – and those in your life – fit in.

1. Did I call a friend I haven't spoken to in a while and share something about them I like or admire? **Yes? No?**

2. Did I meditate for 13 minutes? **Yes? No?** What thoughts came up? Were any of these thoughts recurring?

_____

_____

_____

_____

3. When my thoughts appeared, did I simply notice them with no judgment and use an anchor to return to my breath? **Yes? No?**

4. What anchor(s) did I use? _____

5. Did I feel any tense spots in my body? The meditation I did on Day 5 suggested that I send my breath to any part of my body that is tense, in pain or has fallen asleep. Did I do this? **Yes? No?**

6. Did I take five deep breaths after I told myself twice today, "I love you (my name)?" **Yes? No?**

7. Did I use the Triangle of Self-Awareness during a stressful situation today, which will help me respond rather than react to life's events? **Yes? No?**

8. When I hit a rough patch today, did I repeat the long vowel Eeeeeeee out loud until I laughed? **Yes? No?**

9. Did I notice little things that made me smile? **Yes? No?**

10. Did I tell myself throughout the day: "Today is a happy day and I vow to choose to be happy?" **Yes? No?**

11. Name five happy or pleasant events that filled my day.

a._____

b. _____

c. _____

d._____

e._____

12. How does writing about these events make me feel?

_____

_____

_____

13. Did I practice and/or use the bellows, box and sequence breathing techniques? **Yes? No?**

14. Did I use the STOP meditation? **Yes? No?** Did I do the SAFE meditation? **Yes? No?** Did I find comfort in simply thinking the word *soften*? **Yes? No?**

15. Throughout the day, was I able to relax the muscles in my face, especially around my jaw, neck and shoulders, where tension likes to hang out? Did I pay attention to what happens in my body as I relax? **Yes? No?**

16. My mindful thoughts for the day:

_____

_____

_____

_____

_____

_____

DAY 23

"You were born to be real, not perfect."
– Pathway to Mindfulness

Today you learned one of our favorite stories – polar bear meets the huskie – and how it's a perfect tale to think about when meeting an aggressive personality. You also learned about the beauty of silence.

1. Did I resist the urge to turn on my car radio? **Yes? No?**

2. Did I meditate for 13 minutes? **Yes? No?** What thoughts came up? Were any of these thoughts recurring?

_____

_____

_____

_____

_____

_____

3. When my thoughts appeared, did I simply notice them with no judgment and use an anchor to return to my breath? **Yes? No?**

4. What anchor(s) did I use? _____

5. Did I feel any tense spots in my body? The meditation on Day 5 suggested that I send my breath to a part of my body that is tense, in pain or has fallen asleep. Did I? **Yes? No?**

6. Did I take five deep breaths after I told myself twice today, "I love you (my name)?" **Yes? No?**

7. Did I use the Triangle of Self-Awareness during a stressful situation today, which will help me respond rather than react to life's events? **Yes? No?**

8. When I hit a rough patch today, did I repeat the long vowel Eeeeeeeee out loud until I laughed? **Yes? No?**

9. Did I notice little things that made me smile? **Yes? No?**

10. Did I tell myself throughout the day: "Today is a happy day and I vow to choose to be happy?" **Yes? No?**

11. Name five happy or pleasant events that filled my day.

a._____

b. _____

c. _____

d._____

e._____

12. How does writing about these events make me feel now?

_____

_____

13. Did I practice and/or use the bellows, box and sequence breathing techniques? **Yes? No?**

14. Did I use the STOP meditation? **Yes? No?** Did I do the SAFE meditation? **Yes? No?** Did I find comfort in simply thinking the word *soften*? **Yes? No?**

15. Throughout the day, was I able to relax the muscles in my face, especially around my jaw, neck and shoulders, where tension likes to hang out? Did I pay attention to what happens in my body as I relax? **Yes? No?**

16. My mindful thoughts for the day:

_____

_____

_____

_____

_____

DAY 24

"Be yourself. Everyone else is taken."
— Oscar Wilde

You learned three key questions today:.
- Did you hear what I said or what you thought I was going to say?
- Did you listen with the intent to fix?
- Did you interrupt?

1. Did I diad with a partner? **Yes? No?** If yes, how did It go?

_____

_____

_____

2. Did I meditate for 14 minutes? **Yes? No?** What thoughts came up? Were any of these thoughts recurring?

_____

_____

_____

3. When thoughts appeared, did I notice them with no judgment and use an anchor to return to my breath? **Yes? No?**

4. What anchor(s) did I use? _____

5. Did I send my breath to any part of my body that is tense, in pain or has fallen asleep. **Yes? No?**

6. Did I take five deep breaths after I told myself twice today, "I love you (my name)?" **Yes? No?**

7. Did I use the Triangle of Self-Awareness during a stressful situation today, which will help me respond rather than react to life's events? **Yes? No?**

8. When I hit a rough patch today, did I repeat the long vowel Eeeeeeeee out loud until I laughed? **Yes? No?**

9. Did I notice little things that made me smile? **Yes? No?**

10. Did I tell myself throughout the day: "Today is a happy day and I vow to choose to be happy?" Y**es? No?**

11. Name five happy or pleasant events that filled my day.

a._____

b. _____

c. _____

d._____

e._____

12. How does writing about these events make me feel now?

_____

_____

_____

13. Did I practice and/or use the bellows, box and sequence breathing techniques? **Yes? No?**

14. Did I use the STOP meditation? **Yes? No?** Did I do the SAFE meditation? **Yes? No?** Did I find comfort in simply thinking the word *soften*? **Yes? No?**

15. Did I relax the muscles in my face especially around my jaw, neck and shoulders, where tension likes to hang out? Did I notice what happens in my body as I relax? **Yes? No?**

16. My mindful thoughts for the day:

_____

_____

_____

_____

DAY 25

*"You can only find true happiness when you stop
comparing yourself to others."
– Pathway to Mindfulness*

What did you think about the Microsoft study that found gold-fish have an attention greater than ours? OK – only one second! But still…And that other factoid, that on average our minds wander 53-60 percent of the time.

1. Did I really listen to conversations with others? **Yes? No?**

2. Did I meditate for 14 minutes? **Yes? No?** What thoughts came up? Were any of these thoughts recurring?

_____

_____

_____

3. When thoughts appeared, did I notice them with no judgment and use an anchor to return to my breath? **Yes? No?**

4. What anchor(s) did I use? _____

5. Did I send my breath to any part of my body that is tense, in pain or has fallen asleep. **Yes? No?**

6. Did I take five deep breaths after I told myself twice today, "I love you (my name)?" **Yes? No?**

7. Did I use the Triangle of Self-Awareness during a stressful situation today, which will help me respond rather than react to life's events? **Yes? No?**

8. When I hit a rough patch, did I repeat the long vowel Eeeeeeeee out loud,, until I laughed? **Yes? No?**

9. Did I notice little things that made me smile? **Yes? No?**

10. Did I tell myself throughout the day: "Today is a happy day and I vow to choose to be happy?" **Yes? No?**

11. Name five happy or pleasant events that filled my day.

a._____

b. _____

c. _____

d._____

e._____

12. How does writing about these events make me feel now?

_____

_____

_____

13. Did I practice and/or use the bellows, box and sequence breathing techniques? **Yes? No?**

14. Did I use the STOP meditation? **Yes? No?** Did I do the SAFE meditation? **Yes? No?** Did I find comfort in simply thinking the word *soften*? **Yes? No?**

15. Did I relax the muscles in my face, especially around my jaw, neck and shoulders, where tension likes to hangout? Did I notice what happens in my body as I relax? **Yes? No?**

16. My mindful thoughts for the day:

_____

_____

_____

_____

_____

_____

_____

_____

DAY 26

"It doesn't matter how slowly you go as long as you don't stop." – Confucius

Today you learned about the four communication stages – what you intend to say; what you ultimately say; what the other person hears; what the other person thinks you mean – and how each impacts how successful your conversations become.

1. Did I tell people today that I felt "terrific?" **Yes? No?** How did that make me feel?

_____

_____

_____

2. Did I meditate for 14 minutes? **Yes? No?** What thoughts came up? Were any of these thoughts recurring?

_____

_____

_____

3. When thoughts appeared, did I notice them with no judgment and use an anchor to return to my breath? **Yes? No?**

4. What anchor(s) did I use? _____

5. Did I send my breath to any part of my body that is tense, in pain or has fallen asleep. **Yes? No?**

6. Did I take five deep breaths after I told myself twice today, "I love you (my name)?" **Yes? No?**

7. Did I use the Triangle of Self-Awareness during a stressful situation today? **Yes? No?**

8. When I hit a rough patch today, did I repeat the long vowel Eeeeeeeee out loud, over until I laughed? **Yes? No?**

9. Did I notice little things that made me smile? **Yes? No?**

10. Did I tell myself throughout the day: "Today is a happy day and I vow to choose to be happy?" **Yes? No?**

11. Name five happy or pleasant events that filled my day.

a._____

b. _____

c. _____

d._____

e._____

12. How does writing about these events make me feel now?

_____

_____

_____

13. Did I practice and/or use the bellows, box and sequence breathing techniques? **Yes? No?**

14. Did I use the STOP meditation? **Yes? No?** Did I do the SAFE meditation? **Yes? No?** Did I find comfort in simply thinking the word *soften*? **Yes? No?**

15. Did I relax the muscles in my face, especially around my jaw, neck and shoulders, where tension likes to hang out? Did I notice what happens in my body as I relax? **Yes? No?**

16. My mindful thoughts for the day:

_____

_____

_____

_____

DAY 27

*"About 90 percent of your life is determined
by how you respond to it." – Pathway to Mindfulness*

You learned two beautiful meditations today, both quite simple, and it is this simplicity that makes them important tools on a rough day or when you need a bit of settling.

1. Instead of reaching for something sweet mid-afternoon today, did I take three deep breaths and poll my Triangle of Self-Awareness? Did the breaths help me relax? **Yes? No?**

_____

_____

_____

2. Did I meditate for 15 minutes? **Yes? No?** What thoughts came up? Were any of these thoughts recurring?

_____

_____

_____

3. When thoughts appeared, did I notice them with no judgment and use an anchor to return to my breath? **Yes? No?**

4. What anchor(s) did I use? _____

5. Did I send my breath to any part of my body that is tense, in pain or has fallen asleep. **Yes? No?**

6. Did I take five deep breaths after I told myself twice today, "I love you (my name)?" **Yes? No?**

7. Did I use the Triangle of Self-Awareness during a stressful situation today, which will help me respond rather than react to life's events? **Yes? No?**

8. When I hit a rough patch today, did I repeat the long vowel Eeeeeeeee out loud until I laughed? **Yes? No?**

9. Did I notice little things that made me smile? **Yes? No?**

10. Did I tell myself throughout the day: "Today is a happy day and I vow to choose to be happy?" **Yes? No?**

11. Name five happy or pleasant events that filled my day.

a._____

b. _____

c. _____

d._____

e._____

12. How does writing about these events make me feel now?

_____

_____

13. Did I practice and/or use the bellows, box and sequence breathing techniques? **Yes? No?**

14. Did I use the STOP meditation? **Yes? No?** Did I do the SAFE meditation? **Yes? No?** Did I find comfort in simply thinking the word *soften*? **Yes? No?**

15. Did I relax the muscles in my face today, especially around my jaw, neck and shoulders, where tension likes to hang out? Did I pay attention to what happens in my body as I relax? **Yes? No?**

16. My mindful thoughts for the day:

_____

_____

_____

_____

_____

DAY 28

*"Be kind whenever possible. It is always possible.
– Dalai Lama*

Today you hit the halfway mark, immersed in this mindfulness program that will change your life.

1. Did I re-read and re-commit to my contract? **Yes? No?**

2. Did I meditate for 15 minutes? **Yes? No?** What thoughts came up? Were any of these thoughts recurring?

_____

_____

_____

3. When my thoughts appeared, did I simply notice them with no judgment and use an anchor to return to my breath? **Yes? No?**

4. What anchor(s) did I use? _____

5. Did I feel any tense spots in my body? The meditation I did on Day 5 suggested that I send my breath to any part of my body that is tense, in pain or has fallen asleep. Did I do this? **Yes? No?**

6. Did I take five deep breaths after I told myself twice today, "I love you (my name)?" **Yes? No?**

7. Did I use the Triangle of Self-Awareness during a stressful situation today, which will help me respond rather than react to life's events? **Yes? No?**

8. When I hit a rough patch today, did I repeat the long vowel Eeeeeeeee out loud until I laughed? **Yes? No?**

9. Did I notice little things that made me smile? **Yes? No?**

10. Did I tell myself throughout the day: "Today is a happy day and I vow to choose to be happy?" **Yes? No?**

11. Name five happy or pleasant events that filled my day.

a._____

b. _____

c. _____

d._____

e._____

12. How does writing about these happy events make me feel now?

_____

_____

_____

13. Did I practice and/or use the bellows, box and sequence breathing techniques? **Yes? No?**

14. Did I use the STOP meditation? **Yes? No?** Did I do the SAFE meditation? **Yes? No?** Did I find comfort in simply thinking the word *soften*? **Yes? No?**

15. Did I relax the muscles in my face today, especially around my jaw, neck and shoulders, where tension likes to hang out? Did I pay attention to what happens in my body as I relax? **Yes? No?**

16. My mindful thoughts for the day:

_____

_____

_____

_____

_____

_____

_____

_____

DAY 29

"What is called genius is the abundance of life and health" – Henry David Thoreau

1. Did I find any changes in the Mindful Awareness Survey?

_____

_____

_____

2. Did chewing one bite of food 20 times make my inner critic come out? How?

_____

_____

_____

3. Did I meditate for 15 minutes? **Yes? No?** What thoughts came up? Were any of these thoughts recurring?

_____

_____

_____

4. When thoughts appeared, did I notice them with no judgment and use an anchor to return to my breath? **Yes? No?**

5. What anchor(s) did I use? _____

6. Did I send my breath to any part of my body that is tense, in pain or has fallen asleep. **Yes? No?**

7. Did I take five deep breaths after I told myself twice today, "I love you (my name)?" **Yes? No?**

8. Did I use the Triangle of Self-Awareness to respond rather than react to life's events? **Yes? No?**

9. When I hit a rough patch today, did I repeat the long vowel Eeeeeeeee out loud until I laughed? **Yes? No?**

10. Did I notice little things that made me smile? **Yes? No?**

11. Did I tell myself throughout the day: "Today is a happy day and I vow to choose to be happy?" **Yes? No?**

12. Name five happy or pleasant events that filled my day.

a._____

b. _____

c. _____

d._____

e._____

13. How does writing about these events make me feel now?

_____

_____

_____

14. Did I practice and/or use the bellows, box and sequence breathing techniques? **Yes? No?**

15. Did I use the STOP meditation? **Yes? No?** Did I do the SAFE meditation? **Yes? No?** Did I find comfort in simply thinking the word *soften*? **Yes? No?**

16. Did I relax the muscles in my face today? Did I pay attention to what happens in my body as I relax? **Yes? No?**

17. My mindful thoughts for the day:

_____

_____

_____

_____

_____

_____

DAY 30

"Today is a great day to be happy!"
– Pathway to Mindfulness

1. What personality type(s) defines my inner critic?

_____

_____

_____

2. Did I set alerts to ring throughout the day to serve as reminders to take a few minutes to close my eyes and breathe? **Yes? No?**

3. Did I meditate for 15 minutes? **Yes? No?** What thoughts came up? Were any of these thoughts recurring?

_____

_____

_____

4. When thoughts appeared, did I notice them with no judgment and use an anchor to return to my breath? **Yes? No?**

5. What anchor(s) did I use? _____

6. Did I send my breath to any part of my body that is tense, in pain or has fallen asleep. **Yes? No?**

7. Did I take five deep breaths after I told myself twice today, "I love you (my name)?" **Yes? No?**

8. Did I use the Triangle of Self-Awareness during a stressful situation today, which will help me respond rather than react to life's events? **Yes? No?**

9. When I hit a rough patch today, did I repeat the long vowel Eeeeeeeee out loud until I laughed? **Yes? No?**

10. Did I notice little things that made me smile? **Yes? No?**

11. Did I tell myself throughout the day: "Today is a happy day and I vow to choose to be happy?" **Yes? No?**

12. Name five happy or pleasant events that filled my day.

a._____

b. _____

c. _____

d._____

e._____

13. How does writing about happy events make me feel?

_____

_____

_____

14. Did I practice and/or use the bellows, box and sequence breathing techniques? **Yes? No?**

15. Did I use the STOP meditation? **Yes? No?** Did I do the SAFE meditation? **Yes? No?** Did I find comfort in simply thinking the word *soften*? **Yes? No?**

16. Did I relax the muscles in my face today? Did I pay attention to what happens in my body as I relax? **Yes? No?**

17. My mindful thoughts for the day:

_____

_____

_____

_____

_____

_____

DAY 31

"Today might not be a great day, but if you look really hard, you will find something good."
– Pathway to Mindfulness

1. I learned the RAIN meditation today, which can be so helpful when I am feeling overwhelmed. Is this a meditation that I can see myself using? **Yes? No?**

2. Did I change my environment at lunch today, and really pay attention to what I was eating? **Yes? No?**

3. Did I meditate for 16 minutes? **Yes? No?** What thoughts came up? Were any of these thoughts recurring?

_____

_____

_____

4. When my thoughts appeared, did I simply notice them with no judgment and use an anchor to return to my breath? **Yes? No?**

5. What anchor(s) did I use? _____

6. Did I send my breath to any part of my body that is tense, in pain or has fallen asleep. **Yes? No?**

7. Did I take five deep breaths after I told myself twice today, "I love you (my name)?" **Yes? No?**

8. Did I use the Triangle of Self-Awareness during a stressful situation today, which will help me respond rather than react to life's events? **Yes? No?**

9. When I hit a rough patch today, did I repeat the long vowel Eeeeeeeee out loud until I laughed? **Yes? No?**

10. Did I notice little things that made me smile? **Yes? No?**

11. Did I tell myself throughout the day: "Today is a happy day and I vow to choose to be happy?" **Yes? No?**

12. Name five happy or pleasant events that filled my day.

a._____

b. _____

c. _____

d._____

e._____

13. How does writing about happy events make me feel?

_____

_____

_____

14. Did I practice and/or use the bellows, box and sequence breathing techniques? **Yes? No?**

15. Did I use the STOP meditation? **Yes? No?** Did I do the SAFE meditation? **Yes? No?** Did I find comfort in simply thinking the word *soften*? **Yes? No?**

16. Did I relax the muscles in my face today? Did I pay attention to what happens in my body as I relax? **Yes? No?**

17. My mindful thoughts for the day:

_____

_____

_____

_____

_____

_____

_____

_____

DAY 32

"If you have no expectations, you will never be disappointed." – Pathway to Mindfulness

1. Did I sign the contract with my inner critic? **Yes? No?**

2. Did I write down my positive traits? **Yes? No?**

3. Did I meditate for 16 minutes? **Yes? No?** What thoughts came up? Were any of these thoughts recurring?

_____

_____

_____

4. When thoughts appeared, did I notice them with no judgment and use an anchor to return to my breath? **Yes? No?**

5. What anchor(s) did I use? _____

6. Did I send my breath to any part of my body that is tense, in pain or has fallen asleep. **Yes? No?**

7. Did I take five deep breaths after I told myself twice today, "I love you (my name)?" **Yes? No?**

8. Did I use the Triangle of Self-Awareness during a stressful situation today, which will help me respond rather than react to life's events? **Yes? No?**

9. When I hit a rough patch today, did I repeat the long vowel Eeeeeeeee out loud until I laughed? **Yes? No?**

10. Did I notice little things that made me smile? **Yes? No?**

11. Did I tell myself throughout the day: "Today is a happy day and I vow to choose to be happy?" **Yes? No?**

12. Did I practice and/or use the bellows, box and sequence breathing techniques? **Yes? No?**

13. Did I use the STOP meditation? **Yes? No?** Did I do the SAFE meditation? **Yes? No?** Did I find comfort in simply thinking the word *soften*? **Yes? No?**

14. Did I relax the muscles in my face today? Did I pay attention to what happens in my body as I relax? **Yes? No?**

15. Name five happy or pleasant events that filled my day.

a._____

b. _____

c. _____

d._____

e._____

16. How does writing about these events make me feel now?

_____

_____

_____

17. My mindful thoughts for the day:

_____

_____

_____

_____

_____

_____

_____

_____

_____

_____

DAY 33

"You face choices in life every day. Choose wisely."
– Pathway to Mindfulness

Today we discovered how important, yet difficult, it is to forgive ourselves and others.

1. Can I forgive myself? **Yes? No?** How?

_____

_____

2. Is there someone I have not forgiven? **Yes? No?**

3. Am I willing to forgive this person? **Yes? No?** How?

_____

_____

_____

4. Did I meditate between 16 and 20 minutes? **Yes? No?**
What thoughts came up? Were any thoughts recurring?

_____

_____

_____

5. When thoughts appeared, did I notice them with no judgment and use an anchor to return to my breath? **Yes? No?**

6. What anchor(s) did I use? _____

7. Did I send my breath to any part of my body that is tense, in pain or has fallen asleep. **Yes? No?**

8. Did I take five deep breaths after I told myself twice today, "I love you (my name)?" **Yes? No?**

9. Did I use the Triangle of Self-Awareness during a stressful situation today? **Yes? No?**

10. When I hit a rough patch today, did I repeat the long vowel Eeeeeeeee out loud until I laughed? **Yes? No?**

11. Did I notice little things that made me smile? **Yes? No?**

12. Did I tell myself throughout the day: "Today is a happy day and I vow to choose to be happy?" **Yes? No?**

13. Name five happy or pleasant events that filled my day.

a._____

b. _____

c. _____

d._____

e._____

14. How does writing about these events make me feel now?

_____

_____

_____

15. Did I practice and/or use the bellows, box and sequence breathing techniques? **Yes? No?**

16. Did I use the STOP meditation? **Yes? No?** Did I do the SAFE meditation? **Yes? No?** Did I find comfort in simply thinking the word *soften*? **Yes? No?**

17. Did I relax the muscles in my face today? Did I pay attention to what happens in my body as I relax? **Yes? No?**

18. My mindful thoughts for the day:

_____

_____

_____

DAY 34

"Whatever you do in life, make sure that it is something you want to do, not something someone else wants you to do." – Pathway to Mindfulness

1. Ah, the body scan! Did I like it? **Yes? No?**

2. Did I practice self-care throughout the day? **Yes? No?**

3. Did I make a new recipe? **Yes? No?** Do I like mindful eating? **Yes? No?** If yes, how will I continue to eat mindfully?

_____

_____

4. Did I meditate for 16-20 minutes? **Yes? No?** What thoughts came up? Were any of these thoughts recurring?

_____

_____

_____

5. When thoughts appeared, did I notice them with no judgment and use an anchor to return to my breath? **Yes? No?**

6. What anchor(s) did I use? _____

7. Did I send my breath to any part of my body that is tense, in pain or has fallen asleep. **Yes? No?**

8. Did I take five deep breaths after I told myself twice today, "I love you (my name)?" **Yes? No?**

9. Did I use the Triangle of Self-Awareness during a stressful situation today, which will help me respond rather than react to life's events? **Yes? No?**

10. When I hit a rough patch today, did I repeat the long vowel Eeeeeeeee out loud until I laughed? **Yes? No?**

11. Did I notice little things that made me smile? **Yes? No?**

12. Did I tell myself throughout the day: "Today is a happy day and I vow to choose to be happy?" **Yes? No?**

13. Name five happy or pleasant events that filled my day.

a._____

b. _____

c. _____

d._____

e._____

14. How does writing about these events make me feel now?

_____

_____

_____

15. Did I practice and/or use the bellows, box and sequence breathing techniques? **Yes? No?**

16. Did I use the STOP meditation? **Yes? No?** Did I do the SAFE meditation? **Yes? No?** Did I find comfort in simply thinking the word *soften*? **Yes? No?**

17. Did I relax the muscles in my face today? Did I pay attention to what happens in my body as I relax? **Yes? No?**

18. My mindful thoughts for the day:

_____

_____

_____

_____

_____

_____

_____

_____

DAY 35

*"If you see someone without a smile,
give them one of yours." –Dolly Parton*

1. Did I re-read and re-commit to my contract? **Yes? No?**

2. Did I look at my positive traits list? **Yes? No?**

3. Have I added to my positive traits? **Yes? No?**

4. If no, why not?

_____

_____

_____

5. Did I meditate for 17-20 minutes? **Yes? No?** What thoughts came up? Were any of these thoughts recurring?

_____

_____

_____

6. When thoughts appeared, did I notice them with no judgment and use an anchor to return to my breath? **Yes? No?**

7. What anchor(s) did I use? _____

8. Did I feel send my breath to any part of my body that is tense, in pain or has fallen asleep. **Yes? No?**

9. Did I take five deep breaths after I told myself twice today, "I love you (my name)?" **Yes? No?**

10. Did I use the Triangle of Self-Awareness during a stressful situation today? **Yes? No?**

11. When I hit a rough patch today, did I repeat the long vowel Eeeeeeeee out loud until I laughed? **Yes? No?**

12. Did I notice little things that made me smile? **Yes? No?**

13. Did I tell myself throughout the day: "Today is a happy day and I vow to choose to be happy?" **Yes? No?**

14. Name five happy or pleasant events that filled my day.

a._____

b. _____

c. _____

d._____

e._____

15. How does writing about these events make me feel now?

_____

_____

_____

16. Did I practice and/or use the bellows, box and sequence breathing techniques? **Yes? No?**

17. Did I use the STOP meditation? **Yes? No?** Did I do the SAFE meditation? **Yes? No?** Did I find comfort in simply thinking the word *soften*? **Yes? No?**

18. Did I relax the muscles in my face today? Did I pay attention to what happens in my body as I relax? **Yes? No?**

19. My mindful thoughts for the day:

_____

_____

_____

_____

_____

_____

DAY 36

*"The more you love yourself, the better able
you will be to love others." – Pathway to Mindfulness*

1. Did I do the exercise for turning down my negative thoughts? **Yes? No?**

2. How did it make me feel?

_____

_____

3. Did I meditate for 17-20 minutes? **Yes? No?** What thoughts came up? Were any of these thoughts recurring?

_____

_____

_____

4. When thoughts appeared, did I notice them with no judgment and use an anchor to return to my breath? **Yes? No?**

5. What anchor(s) did I use? _____

6. Did I send my breath to any part of my body that is tense, in pain or has fallen asleep.**Yes? No?**

7. Did I take five deep breaths after I told myself twice today, "I love you (my name)?" **Yes? No?**

8. Did I use the Triangle of Self-Awareness during a stressful situation today? **Yes? No?**

9. When I hit a rough patch today, did I repeat the long vowel Eeeeeeee out loud until I laughed? **Yes? No?**

10. Did I notice little things that made me smile? **Yes? No?**

11. Did I tell myself throughout the day: "Today is a happy day and I vow to choose to be happy?" **Yes? No?**

12. Name five happy or pleasant events that filled my day.

a._____

b. _____

c. _____

d._____

e._____

13. How does writing about these events make me feel now?

_____

_____

_____

14. Did I practice and/or use the bellows, box and sequence breathing techniques? **Yes? No?**

15. Did I use the STOP meditation? **Yes? No?** Did I do the SAFE meditation? **Yes? No?** Did I find comfort in simply thinking the word *soften*? **Yes? No?**

16. Did I relax the muscles in my face today? Did I pay attention to what happens in my body as I relax? **Yes? No?**

17. Did I read and/or add to my positive traits list? **Yes? No?**

18. My mindful thoughts for the day:

_____

_____

_____

_____

_____

_____

_____

_____

DAY 37

"Be brave enough to be bad at something new. Take chances. Spread your wings." – Pathway to Mindfulness

The vagus nerve truly is spectacular – stimulating and strengthening soothing hormones such as oxytocin, and happy hormones, including dopamine and endorphins.

1. What simple act of kindness did I do today?

_____

_____

_____

2. Did I meditate for 17-20 minutes? **Yes? No?** What thoughts came up? Were any of these thoughts recurring?

_____

_____

_____

3. When thoughts appeared, did I notice them with no judgment and use an anchor to return to my breath? **Yes? No?**

4. What anchor(s) did I use? _____

5. Did I send my breath to any part of my body that is tense, in pain or has fallen asleep. **Yes? No?**

6. Did I take five deep breaths after I told myself twice today, "I love you (my name)?" **Yes? No?**

7. Did I use the Triangle of Self-Awareness during a stressful situation today? **Yes? No?**

8. When I hit a rough patch today, did I repeat the long vowel Eeeeeeeee out loud until I laughed? **Yes? No?**

9. Did I notice little things that made me smile? **Yes? No?**

10. Did I tell myself throughout the day: "Today is a happy day and I vow to choose to be happy?" **Yes? No?**

11. Name five happy or pleasant events that filled my day.

a._____

b. _____

c. _____

d._____

e._____

12. How does writing about these events make me feel now?

_____

_____

_____

13. Did I practice and/or use the bellows, box and sequence breathing techniques? **Yes? No?**

14. Did I use the STOP meditation? **Yes? No?** Did I do the SAFE meditation? **Yes? No?** Did I find comfort in simply thinking the word *soften*? **Yes? No?**

15. Did I relax the muscles in my face today? Did I pay attention to what happens in my body as I relax? **Yes? No?**

16. Did I read and/or add to my positive traits list? **Yes? No?**

17. My mindful thoughts for the day:

_____

_____

_____

_____

_____

_____

DAY 38

"Until you stop caring about what others think of you, you are a prisoner of others." – Pathway to Mindfulness

Today we talked about loving kindness – and the importance of loving yourself so that you can love others.

1. Did I meditate for 17-20 minutes? **Yes? No?** What thoughts came up? Were any of these thoughts recurring?

_____

_____

_____

2. What anchor(s) did I use?_____

3. Did I take five deep breaths after I told myself twice today, "I love you (my name)?" **Yes? No?**

4. Did I use the Triangle of Self-Awareness during a stressful situation today, to respond rather than react? **Yes? No?**

5. When I hit a rough patch today, did I repeat the long vowel Eeeeeeeee out loud until I laughed? **Yes? No?**

6. Did I notice little things that made me smile? **Yes? No?**

7. Did I tell myself throughout the day: "Today is a happy day and I vow to choose to be happy?" **Yes? No?**

8. Name five happy or pleasant events that filled my day.

a._____

b. _____

c. _____

d._____

e._____

9. Did I practice and/or use the bellows, box and sequence breathing techniques? **Yes? No?**

10. Did I use the STOP meditation? **Yes? No?** Did I do the SAFE meditation? **Yes? No?** Did I find comfort in simply thinking the word *soften*? **Yes? No?**

11. Did I relax the muscles in my face today? Did I pay attention to what happens in my body as I relax? **Yes? No?**

12 Did I read and/or add to my positive traits list? **Yes? No?**

13. What nourished me today?

_____

_____

_____

14. What depleted my energy today?

_____

_____

_____

15. What can I let go of?

_____

_____

_____

16. My mindful thoughts for the day:

_____

_____

_____

_____

_____

_____

_____

DAY 39

"You yourself, as much as anybody in the entire universe, deserve your love and attention." – Buddha

Today we delved a little deeper into self-care and shared mindfulness teacher Thich Nhat Hanh's expanded definition of diet to not only include what we eat and drink but what we consume with all our senses.

1. Did I meditate for 18-20 minutes? **Yes? No?** What thoughts came up? Were any of these thoughts recurring?

_____

_____

_____

2. What anchor(s) did I use?_____

3. Did I take five deep breaths after I told myself twice today, "I love you (my name)?" **Yes? No?**

4. Did I use the Triangle of Self-Awareness during a stressful situation today, to respond rather than react? **Yes? No?**

5. When I hit a rough patch today, did I repeat the long vowel Eeeeeeeee out loud until I laughed? **Yes? No?**

6. Did I notice little things that made me smile? **Yes? No?**

7. Did I tell myself throughout the day: "Today is a happy day and I vow to choose to be happy?" **Yes? No?**

8. Name five happy or pleasant events that filled my day.

a._____

b._____

c._____

d._____

e._____

9. Did I use bellows, box and sequence breaths? **Yes? No?**

10. Did I use the STOP meditation? **Yes? No?** Did I do the SAFE meditation? **Yes? No?** Did I find comfort in simply thinking the word *soften*? **Yes? No?**

11. Did I relax the muscles in my face today? Did I pay attention to what happens in my body as I relax? **Yes? No?**

12 Did I read and/or add to my positive traits list? **Yes? No?**

13. What nourished me today?

_____

_____

14. What depleted my energy today?

_____

_____

15. What can I let go of?

_____

_____

16. What are the stressors in my life?

_____

_____

_____

17. My mindful thoughts for the day:

_____

_____

_____

_____

DAY 40

"Your Triangle of Self-Awareness is an important tool for leading a mindful life." – Pathway to Mindfulness

1. Did I meditate for 18-20 minutes? **Yes? No?** What thoughts came up? Were any of these thoughts recurring?

_____

_____

_____

2. What anchor(s) did I use?_____

3. Did I take five deep breaths after I told myself twice today, "I love you (my name)?" **Yes? No?**

4. Did I use the Triangle of Self-Awareness during a stressful situation today, to respond rather than react? **Yes? No?**

5. When I hit a rough patch today, did I repeat the long vowel Eeeeeeeee out loud until I laughed? **Yes? No?**

6. Did I notice little things that made me smile? **Yes? No?**

7. Did I tell myself throughout the day: "Today is a happy day and I vow to choose to be happy?" **Yes? No?**

8. Name five happy or pleasant events that filled my day.

a._____

b. _____

c. _____

d._____

e._____

9. Did I use bellows, box and sequence breaths? **Yes? No?**

10. Did I use the STOP meditation? **Yes? No?** Did I do the SAFE meditation? **Yes? No?** Did I find comfort in simply thinking the word *soften*? **Yes? No?**

11. Did I relax the muscles in my face today? Did I pay attention to what happens in my body as I relax? **Yes? No?**

12 Did I read and/or add to my positive traits list? **Yes? No?**

13. What nourished me today?

_____

_____

_____

14. What depleted my energy today?

_____

_____

_____

15. What can I let go of?

_____

_____

_____

16. What are the stressors in my life?

_____

_____

_____

17. My mindful thoughts for the day:

_____

_____

_____

_____

_____

DAY 41

*"It is so easy to doubt ourselves. What is hard
is keeping self-doubt from propelling us forward."
– Pathway to Mindfulness*

1. Did I meditate for 18-20 minutes? **Yes? No?** What
thoughts came up? Were any of these thoughts recurring?

_____

_____

_____

2. What anchor(s) did I use?_____

3. Did I take five deep breaths after I told myself twice today,
"I love you (my name)?" **Yes? No?**

4. Did I use the Triangle of Self-Awareness during a stressful
situation today, to respond rather than react? **Yes? No?**

5. When I hit a rough patch today, did I repeat the long vowel
Eeeeeeeee out loud until I laughed? **Yes? No?**

6. Did I notice little things that made me smile? **Yes? No?**

7. Did I tell myself throughout the day: "Today is a happy day
and I vow to choose to be happy?" **Yes? No?**

8. Name five happy or pleasant events that filled my day.

a._____

b. _____

c. _____

d._____

e._____

9. Did I practice and/or use the bellows, box and sequence
breathing techniques? **Yes? No?**

10. Did I use the STOP meditation? **Yes? No?** Did I do the SAFE meditation? **Yes? No?** Did I find comfort in simply thinking the word *soften*? **Yes? No?**

11. Did I relax the muscles in my face today? Did I pay attention to what happens in my body as I relax? **Yes? No?**

12 Did I read and/or add to my positive traits list? **Yes? No?**

13. What nourished me today?

_____

_____

_____

14. What depleted my energy today?

_____

_____

_____

15. What can I let go of?

_____

_____

_____

16. What are the stressors in my life?

_____

_____

_____

17. My mindful thoughts for the day:

_____

_____

_____

DAY 42

"Success is not about what you do occasionally but what you do consistently." – Pathway to Mindfulness

1. Did I re-read and re-commit to my contract? **Yes? No?**

2. Did I meditate for 19-20 minutes? **Yes? No?** What thoughts came up? Were any of these thoughts recurring?

_____

_____

_____

3. What anchor(s) did I use?_____

4. Did I take five deep breaths after I told myself twice today, "I love you (my name)?" **Yes? No?**

5. Did I use the Triangle of Self-Awareness during a stressful situation today, to respond rather than react? **Yes? No?**

6. When I hit a rough patch today, did I repeat the long vowel Eeeeeeeee out loud until I laughed? **Yes? No?**

7. Did I notice little things that made me smile? **Yes? No?**

8. Did I tell myself throughout the day: "Today is a happy day and I vow to choose to be happy?" **Yes? No?**

9. Name five happy or pleasant events that filled my day.

a._____

b. _____

c. _____

d._____

e._____

10. Did I practice and/or use the bellows, box and sequence breathing techniques? **Yes? No?**

11. Did I use the STOP meditation? **Yes? No?** Did I do the SAFE meditation? **Yes? No?** Did I find comfort in simply thinking the word *soften*? **Yes? No?**

12. Did I relax the muscles in my face today? Did I pay attention to what happens in my body as I relax? **Yes? No?**

13 Did I read and/or add to my positive traits list? **Yes? No?**

14. What nourished me today?

_____

_____

15. What depleted my energy today?

_____

_____

16. What can I let go of?

_____

_____

_____

17. What are the stressors in my life?

_____

_____

_____

18. My mindful thoughts for the day:

_____

_____

_____

_____

_____

DAY 43

"Do something this week that your future self will thank you for – forever." – Pathway to Mindfulness

1. What did I discover when I used my 20 spoons?

_____

_____

_____

2. Did I meditate for 19-20 minutes? **Yes? No?** What thoughts came up? Were any of these thoughts recurring?

_____

_____

_____

3. What anchor(s) did I use?_____

4. Did I take five deep breaths after I told myself twice today, "I love you (my name)?" **Yes? No?**

5. Did I use the Triangle of Self-Awareness during a stressful situation today, to respond rather than react? **Yes? No?**

6. Did I use bellows, box and sequence breaths? **Yes? No?**

7. Did I use the STOP meditation? **Yes? No?** Did I do the SAFE meditation? **Yes? No?** Did I find comfort in simply thinking the word *soften*? **Yes? No?**

8. Did I relax the muscles in my face today? Did I pay attention to what happens in my body as I relax? **Yes? No?**

9. Did I read and/or add to my positive traits list? **Yes? No?**

10. When I hit a rough patch today, did I repeat the long vowel Eeeeeeeee out loud until I laughed? **Yes? No?**

11. Did I notice little things that made me smile? **Yes? No?**

12. Did I tell myself throughout the day: "Today is a happy day and I vow to choose to be happy?" **Yes? No?**

13. Name five happy or pleasant events that filled my day.

a._____

b. _____

c. _____

d._____

e._____

14. What nourished me today?

_____

_____

15. What depleted my energy today?

_____

_____

16. What can I let go of?

_____

_____

17. What are the stressors in my life?

_____

_____

18. My mindful thoughts for the day:

_____

_____

_____

_____

DAY 44

"A mind is like a parachute. It won't work unless it's open." – Anonymous

1. When I was stressed today, did I thank my body for doing its job? **Yes? No?**

2. Did I meditate for 19-20 minutes? **Yes? No?** What thoughts came up? Were any of these thoughts recurring?

_____

_____

_____

3. What anchor(s) did I use?_____

4. Did I take five deep breaths after I told myself twice today, "I love you (my name)?" **Yes? No?**

5. Did I use the Triangle of Self-Awareness during a stressful situation today, to respond rather than react? **Yes? No?**

6. When I hit a rough patch today, did I repeat the long vowel Eeeeeeee out loud until I laughed? **Yes? No?**

7. Did I notice little things that made me smile? **Yes? No?**

8. Did I tell myself throughout the day: "Today is a happy day and I vow to choose to be happy?" **Yes? No?**

9. Name five happy or pleasant events that filled my day.

a._____

b. _____

c. _____

d._____

e._____

10. Did I use bellows, box and sequence breaths? **Yes? No?**

11. Did I use the STOP meditation? **Yes? No?** Did I do the SAFE meditation? **Yes? No?** Did I find comfort in simply thinking the word *soften*? **Yes? No?**

12. Did I relax the muscles in my face today? Did I pay attention to what happens in my body as I relax? **Yes? No?**

13. Did I read and/or add to my positive traits list? **Yes? No?**

14. What nourished me today?

_____

_____

15. What depleted my energy today?

_____

_____

16. What can I let go of?

_____

_____

17. What are the stressors in my life?

_____

_____

18. My mindful thoughts for the day:

_____

_____

_____

_____

_____

_____

DAY 45

"Acceptance helps you work through each unpleasant experience." – Pathway to Mindfulness

1. Throughout the day, as my heart began to race or my forehead and shoulders started tensing, did I take five deep breaths and poll my Triangle of Self-Awareness? **Yes? No?**

2. Did I meditate for 19-20 minutes? **Yes? No?** What thoughts came up? Were any of these thoughts recurring?

_____

_____

_____

_____

3. What anchor(s) did I use?_____

4. Did I take five deep breaths after I told myself twice today, "I love you (my name)?" **Yes? No?**

5. Did I use the Triangle of Self-Awareness during a stressful situation today, to respond rather than react? **Yes? No?**

6. When I hit a rough patch today, did I repeat the long vowel Eeeeeeeee out loud until I laughed? **Yes? No?**

7. Did I notice little things that made me smile? **Yes? No?**

8. Did I tell myself throughout the day: "Today is a happy day and I vow to choose to be happy?" **Yes? No?**

9. Name five happy or pleasant events that filled my day.

a._____

b. _____

c. _____

d._____

e._____

10. Did I practice and/or use the bellows, box and sequence breathing techniques? **Yes? No?**

11. Did I use the STOP meditation? **Yes? No?** Did I do the SAFE meditation? **Yes? No?** Did I find comfort in simply thinking the word *soften*? **Yes? No?**

12. Did I relax the muscles in my face today? Did I pay attention to what happens in my body as I relax? **Yes? No?**

13. Did I read and/or add to my positive traits list? **Yes? No?**

14. What nourished me today?

_____

_____

15. What depleted my energy today?

_____

_____

16. What can I let go of?

_____

_____

17. What are the stressors in my life?

_____

_____

18. My mindful thoughts for the day:

_____

_____

_____

_____

DAY 46

"That nothing is static or fixed, that all is fleeting and impermanent, is the first mark of existence."
– Pema Chödron

1. When I wrote of something in my life that is impermanent, was this a good or bad change? **Good? Bad?** How is it affecting my thoughts, emotions and physical sensations?

_____

_____

2. Did I meditate for 19-20 minutes? **Yes? No?** What thoughts came up? Were any of these thoughts recurring?

_____

_____

_____

3. What anchor(s) did I use?_____

4. Did I take five deep breaths after I told myself twice today, "I love you (my name)?" **Yes? No?**

5. Did I use the Triangle of Self-Awareness during a stressful situation today, to respond rather than react? **Yes? No?**

6. Did I use bellows, box and sequence breaths? **Yes? No?**

7. Did I use the STOP meditation? **Yes? No?** Did I do the SAFE meditation? **Yes? No?** Did I find comfort in simply thinking the word *soften*? **Yes? No?**

8. Did I relax the muscles in my face today? Did I pay attention to what happens in my body as I relax? **Yes? No?**

9. Did I read and/or add to my positive traits list? **Yes? No?**

10. When I hit a rough patch today, did I repeat the long vowel Eeeeeeeee out loud until I laughed? **Yes? No?**

11. Did I notice little things that made me smile? **Yes? No?**

12. Did I tell myself throughout the day: "Today is a happy day and I vow to choose to be happy?" **Yes? No?**

13. Name five happy or pleasant events that filled my day.

a._____

b. _____

c. _____

d._____

e._____

14. What nourished me today?

_____

_____

15. What depleted my energy today?

_____

_____

16. What can I let go of?

_____

_____

17. What are the stressors in my life?

_____

_____

18. My mindful thoughts for the day:

_____

_____

_____

DAY 47

"No man ever steps in the same river twice, for it's not the same river and he's not the same man."
– Heraclitus, pre-Socratic Ionian Greek philosopher

1. When I spoke with someone today, what happened when I asked myself if I am experiencing equanimity?

_____

_____

2. Did I meditate for 20 minutes? **Yes? No?** What thoughts came up? Were any of these thoughts recurring?

_____

_____

_____

3. What anchor(s) did I use?_____

4. Did I take five deep breaths after I told myself twice today, "I love you (my name)?" **Yes? No?**

5. Did I use the Triangle of Self-Awareness during a stressful situation today, to respond rather than react? **Yes? No?**

6. Did I use bellows, box and sequence breaths? **Yes? No?**

7. Did I use the STOP meditation? **Yes? No?** Did I do the SAFE meditation? **Yes? No?** Did I find comfort in simply thinking the word *soften*? **Yes? No?**

8. Did I relax the muscles in my face today? Did I pay attention to what happens in my body as I relax? **Yes? No?**

9. Did I read and/or add to my positive traits list? **Yes? No?**

10. When I hit a rough patch today, did I repeat the long vowel Eeeeeeeee out loud until I laughed? **Yes? No?**

11. Did I notice little things that made me smile? **Yes? No?**

12. Did I tell myself throughout the day: "Today is a happy day and I vow to choose to be happy?" **Yes? No?**

13. Name five happy or pleasant events that filled my day.

a._____

b. _____

c. _____

d._____

e._____

14. What nourished me today?

_____

_____

15. What depleted my energy today?

_____

_____

16. What can I let go of?

_____

_____

17. What are the stressors in my life?

_____

_____

18. My mindful thoughts for the day:

_____

_____

_____

_____

DAY 48

"It is not joy that makes us grateful. It is being grateful that brings us joy." – Pathway to Mindfulness

1. Did I meditate for 20 minutes? **Yes? No?** What thoughts came up? Were any of these thoughts recurring?

_____

_____

_____

2. What anchor(s) did I use?_____

3. Did I take five deep breaths after I told myself today "I love you (my name)?" **Yes? No?**

4. Did I use the Triangle of Self-Awareness during a stressful situation today, to respond rather than react? **Yes? No?**

5. When I hit a rough patch today, did I repeat the long vowel Eeeeeeeee out loud until I laughed? **Yes? No?**

6. Did I notice little things that made me smile? **Yes? No?**

7. Did I tell myself throughout the day: "Today is a happy day and I vow to choose to be happy?" **Yes? No?**

8. Name five happy or pleasant events that filled my day.

a._____

b. _____

c. _____

d._____

e._____

9.Did I use bellows, box and sequence breaths? **Yes? No?**

10. Did I use the STOP meditation? **Yes? No?** Did I do the SAFE meditation? **Yes? No?** Did I find comfort in simply thinking the word *soften*? **Yes? No?**

11. Did I relax the muscles in my face today? Did I pay attention to what happens in my body as I relax? **Yes? No?**

12. Did I read and/or add to my positive traits list? **Yes? No?**

13. What nourished me today?

_____

_____

14. What depleted my energy today?

_____

_____

15. What can I let go of?

_____

_____

16. What are the stressors in my life?

_____

_____

17. What was I grateful for today?

_____

_____

18. My mindful thoughts for the day:

_____

_____

_____

_____

_____

DAY 49

*"Mindfulness lets you fall in love with life,
embracing the little things that once went unnoticed."
– Pathway to Mindfulness*

1. Did I re-read and re-commit to my contract? **Yes? No?**

2. Did I meditate for 20 minutes? **Yes? No?** What thoughts came up? Were any of these thoughts recurring?

_____

_____

_____

_____

3. What anchor(s) did I use?_____

4. Did I take five deep breaths after I told myself twice today, "I love you (my name)?" **Yes? No?**

5. Did I use the Triangle of Self-Awareness during a stressful situation today, to respond rather than react? **Yes? No?**

6. When I hit a rough patch today, did I repeat the long vowel Eeeeeeeee out loud until I laughed? **Yes? No?**

7. Did I notice little things that made me smile? **Yes? No?**

8. Did I tell myself throughout the day: "Today is a happy day and I vow to choose to be happy?" **Yes? No?**

9. Name five happy or pleasant events that filled my day.

a._____

b. _____

c. _____

d._____

e._____

10. Did I use bellows, box and sequence breaths? **Yes? No?**

11. Did I use the STOP meditation? **Yes? No?** Did I do the SAFE meditation? **Yes? No?** Did I find comfort in simply thinking the word *soften*? **Yes? No?**

12. Did I relax the muscles in my face today? Did I pay attention to what happens in my body as I relax? **Yes? No?**

13. Did I read and/or add to my positive traits list? **Yes? No?**

14. What nourished me today?

_____

_____

15. What depleted my energy today?

_____

_____

16. What can I let go of?

_____

_____

17. What are the stressors in my life?

_____

_____

18. What was I grateful for today?

_____

_____

19. My mindful thoughts for the day:

_____

_____

_____

DAY 50

"Don't trade authenticity for approval."
– Pathway to Mindfulness

1. Did I meditate for 20 minutes? **Yes? No?** What thoughts came up? Were any of these thoughts recurring?

_____

_____

_____

_____

2. What anchor(s) did I use?_____

3. Did I take five deep breaths after I told myself twice today, "I love you (my name)?" **Yes? No?**

4. Did I use the Triangle of Self-Awareness during a stressful situation today, to respond rather than react? **Yes? No?**

5. When I hit a rough patch today, did I repeat the long vowel Eeeeeeeee out loud until I laughed? **Yes? No?**

6. Did I notice little things that made me smile? **Yes? No?**

7. Did I tell myself throughout the day: "Today is a happy day and I vow to choose to be happy?" **Yes? No?**

8. Name five happy or pleasant events that filled my day.

a._____

b. _____

c. _____

d._____

e._____

9. Did I use bellows, box and sequence breaths? **Yes? No?**

10. Did I use the STOP meditation? **Yes? No?** Did I do the SAFE meditation? **Yes? No?** Did I find comfort in simply thinking the word *soften*? **Yes? No?**

11. Did I relax the muscles in my face today? Did I pay attention to what happens in my body as I relax? **Yes? No?**

12. Did I read and/or add to my positive traits list? **Yes? No?**

13. What nourished me today?

_____

_____

14. What depleted my energy today?

_____

_____

15. What can I let go of?

_____

_____

16. What are the stressors in my life?

_____

_____

17. What was I grateful for today?

_____

_____

18. My mindful thoughts for the day:

_____

_____

_____

DAY 51

"Can we judge? Maybe a better question would be: Is it possible not to judge?" – Pathway to Mindfulness

1. Did I meditate for 20 minutes? **Yes? No?** What thoughts came up? Were any of these thoughts recurring?

_____

_____

_____

2. What anchor(s) did I use?_____

3. Did I take five deep breaths after I told myself twice today, "I love you (my name)?" **Yes? No?**

4. Did I use the Triangle of Self-Awareness during a stressful situation today, to respond rather than react? **Yes? No?**

5. When I hit a rough patch today, did I repeat the long vowel Eeeeeeeee out loud until I laughed? **Yes? No?**

6. Did I notice little things that made me smile? **Yes? No?**

7. Did I tell myself throughout the day: "Today is a happy day and I vow to choose to be happy?" **Yes? No?**

8. Name five happy or pleasant events that filled my day.

a._____

b. _____

c. _____

d._____

e._____

9. Did I use bellows, box and sequence breaths? **Yes? No?**

10. Did I use the STOP meditation? **Yes? No?** Did I do the SAFE meditation? **Yes? No?** Did I find comfort in simply thinking the word *soften*? **Yes? No?**

11. Did I relax the muscles in my face today? Did I pay attention to what happens in my body as I relax? **Yes? No?**

12. Did I read and/or add to my positive traits list? **Yes? No?**

13. What nourished me today?

_____

_____

14. What depleted my energy today?

_____

_____

15. What can I let go of?

_____

_____

16. What are the stressors in my life?

_____

_____

17. What was I grateful for today?

_____

_____

18. Did I judge today? **Yes? No?** Should I have judged? **Yes? No?**

19. My mindful thoughts for the day:

_____

_____

_____

DAY 52

"Mindfulness is a key element in bringing awe into your daily life." – Pathway to Mindfulness

1. Did I meditate for 20 minutes? **Yes? No?** What thoughts came up? Were any of these thoughts recurring?

_____

_____

_____

2. What anchor(s) did I use?_____

3. Did I take five deep breaths after I told myself twice today, "I love you (my name)?" **Yes? No?**

4. Did I use the Triangle of Self-Awareness during a stressful situation today, to respond rather than react? **Yes? No?**

5. When I hit a rough patch today, did I repeat the long vowel Eeeeeeeee out loud until I laughed? **Yes? No?**

6. Did I notice little things that made me smile? **Yes? No?**

7. Did I tell myself throughout the day: "Today is a happy day and I vow to choose to be happy?" **Yes? No?**

8. Name five happy or pleasant events that filled my day.

a._____

b. _____

c. _____

d._____

e._____

9. Did I use bellows, box and sequence breaths? **Yes? No?**

10. Did I use the STOP meditation? **Yes? No?** Did I do the SAFE meditation? **Yes? No?** Did I find comfort in simply thinking the word *soften*? **Yes? No?**

11. Did I relax the muscles in my face today? Did I pay attention to what happens in my body as I relax? **Yes? No?**

12. Did I read and/or add to my positive traits list? **Yes? No?**

13. What nourished me today?_____

_____

14. What depleted my energy today? _____

_____

15. What can I let go of? _____

_____

16. What are the stressors in my life? _____

_____

17. What was I grateful for today?

_____

_____

18. Did I judge? **Yes? No?** Should I have? **Yes? No?**

19. Did I bring awe into my life today? **Yes? No?** How?

_____

_____

20. My mindful thoughts for the day:

_____

_____

_____

DAY 53

> *"How many times have you said yes when you really meant no?" – Pathway to Mindfulness*

1. Did I meditate for 20 minutes? **Yes? No?** What thoughts came up? Were any of these thoughts recurring?

_____

_____

_____

2. What anchor(s) did I use?_____

3. Did I take five deep breaths after I told myself twice today, "I love you (my name)?" **Yes? No?**

4. Did I use the Triangle of Self-Awareness during a stressful situation today, to respond rather than react? **Yes? No?**

5. When I hit a rough patch today, did I repeat the long vowel Eeeeeeee out loud until I laughed? **Yes? No?**

6. Did I notice little things that made me smile? **Yes? No?**

7. Did I tell myself throughout the day: "Today is a happy day and I vow to choose to be happy?" **Yes? No?**

8. Name five happy or pleasant events that filled my day.

a._____

b. _____

c. _____

d._____

e._____

9. Did I use bellows, box and sequence breaths? **Yes? No?**

10. Did I use the STOP meditation? **Yes? No?** Did I do the SAFE meditation? **Yes? No?** Did I find comfort in simply thinking the word *soften*? **Yes? No?**

11. Did I relax the muscles in my face today? Did I pay attention to what happens in my body as I relax? **Yes? No?**

12. Did I read and/or add to my positive traits list? **Yes? No?**

13. What nourished me today?_____

_____

14. What depleted my energy today? _____

_____

15. What can I let go of? _____

_____

16. What are the stressors in my life? _____

_____

17. What was I grateful for today?

_____

_____

18. Did I judge today? **Yes? No?** Should I have? **Yes? No?**

19. Did I bring awe into my life today? **Yes? No?** If yes, how?

_____

_____

_____

20. Make tomorrow's to-do list, writing yes if it's something you should do or no if it doesn't fit into your life's purpose.

_____

_____

_____

_____

_____

_____

_____

_____

_____

_____

21. My mindful thoughts for the day:

_____

_____

_____

_____

_____

_____

_____

_____

_____

_____

_____

DAY 54

> *"Who has no expectations is rarely disappointed."*
> *– Dr. Lo*

1. Did I meditate for 20 minutes? **Yes? No?** What thoughts came up? Were any of these thoughts recurring?

_____

_____

2. What anchor(s) did I use?_____

3. Did I take five deep breaths after I told myself twice today, "I love you (my name)?" **Yes? No?**

4. Did I use the Triangle of Self-Awareness during a stressful situation today, to respond rather than react? **Yes? No?**

5. When I hit a rough patch today, did I repeat the long vowel Eeeeeeeee out loud until I laughed? **Yes? No?**

6. Did I notice little things that made me smile? **Yes? No?**

7. Did I tell myself throughout the day: "Today is a happy day and I vow to choose to be happy?" **Yes? No?**

8. Name five happy or pleasant events that filled my day.

a._____

b. _____

c. _____

d._____

e._____

9. Did I practice and/or use the bellows, box and sequence breathing techniques? **Yes? No?**

10. Did I use the STOP meditation? **Yes? No?** Did I do the SAFE meditation? **Yes? No?** Did I find comfort in simply thinking the word *soften*? **Yes? No?**

11. Did I relax the muscles in my face today? Did I pay attention to what happens in my body as I relax? **Yes? No?**

12. Did I read and/or add to my positive traits list? **Yes? No?**

13. What nourished me today?

_____

_____

14. What depleted my energy today?

_____

_____

15. What can I let go of?

_____

_____

16. What are the stressors in my life?

_____

_____

17. What was I grateful for today?

_____

_____

18. Did I judge today? **Yes? No?** Should I have judged? **Yes? No?**

19. Did I bring awe into my life today? **Yes? No?** If yes, how?

_____

_____

_____

_____

20. Make tomorrow's to-do list, writing yes if it's something you should do or no if it doesn't fit into your life's purpose.

_____

_____

_____

_____

_____

_____

_____

_____

_____

_____

_____

21. My mindful thoughts for the day:

_____

_____

_____

_____

_____

_____

_____

_____

_____

_____

_____

_____

DAY 55

"Think of mindfulness and curiosity as BFFs."
– Pathway to Mindfulness

1. Did I meditate for 20 minutes? **Yes? No?** What thoughts came up? Were any of these thoughts recurring?

_____

_____

2. What anchor(s) did I use?_____

3. Did I take five deep breaths after I told myself twice today, "I love you (my name)?" **Yes? No?**

4. Did I use the Triangle of Self-Awareness during a stressful situation today, to respond rather than react? **Yes? No?**

5. When I hit a rough patch today, did I repeat the long vowel Eeeeeeee out loud until I laughed? **Yes? No?**

6. Did I notice little things that made me smile? **Yes? No?**

7. Did I tell myself throughout the day: "Today is a happy day and I vow to choose to be happy?" **Yes? No?**

8. Name five happy or pleasant events that filled my day.

a._____

b. _____

c. _____

d._____

e._____

9. Did I use bellows, box and sequence breaths? **Yes? No?**

10. Did I use the STOP meditation? **Yes? No?** Did I do the SAFE meditation? **Yes? No?** Did I find comfort in simply thinking the word *soften*? **Yes? No?**

11. Did I relax the muscles in my face today? Did I pay attention to what happens in my body as I relax? **Yes? No?**

12. Did I read and/or add to my positive traits list? **Yes? No?**

13. What nourished me today?

_____

_____

14. What depleted my energy today?

_____

_____

15. What can I let go of?

_____

_____

16. What are the stressors in my life?

_____

_____

17. What was I grateful for today?

_____

_____

18. Did I judge today? **Yes? No?** Should I have judged? **Yes? No?**

19. Did I bring awe into my life today? **Yes? No?** How?

_____

_____

_____

20. Make tomorrow's to-do list, writing yes if it's something you should do or no if it doesn't fit into your life's purpose.

_____

_____

_____

_____

_____

_____

_____

_____

_____

_____

21. My mindful thoughts for the day:

_____

_____

_____

_____

_____

_____

_____

_____

_____

_____

_____

DAY 56

*"Leading a mindful life is a journey
not a destination and the Pathway to Mindfulness
can take many twists and turns."*

1. Did I meditate for 20 minutes? **Yes? No?** What thoughts came up? Were any of these thoughts recurring?

_____

_____

_____

2. What anchor(s) did I use?_____

3. Did I take five deep breaths after I told myself twice today, "I love you (my name)?" **Yes? No?**

4. Did I use the Triangle of Self-Awareness during a stressful situation today, to respond rather than react? **Yes? No?**

5. When I hit a rough patch today, did I repeat the long vowel Eeeeeeeee out loud until I laughed? **Yes? No?**

6. Did I notice little things that made me smile? **Yes? No?**

7. Did I tell myself throughout the day: "Today is a happy day and I vow to choose to be happy?" **Yes? No?**

8. Name five happy or pleasant events that filled my day.

a._____

b._____

c._____

d._____

e._____

9. Did I use bellows, box and sequence breaths? **Yes? No?**

10. Did I use the STOP meditation? **Yes? No?** Did I do the SAFE meditation? **Yes? No?** Did I find comfort in simply thinking the word *soften*? **Yes? No?**

11. Did I relax the muscles in my face today? Did I pay attention to what happens in my body as I relax? **Yes? No?**

12. Did I read and/or add to my positive traits list? **Yes? No?**

13. What nourished me today?_____

_____

14. What depleted my energy today? _____

_____

15. What can I let go of? _____

_____

16. What are the stressors in my life?

_____

_____

17. What was I grateful for today?

_____

_____

18. Did I judge? **Yes? No?** Should I have judged? **Yes? No?**

19. Did I bring awe into my life today? **Yes? No?** How?

_____

_____

_____

_____

20. Make tomorrow's to-do list, writing yes if it's something you should do or no if it doesn't fit into your life's purpose.

_____

_____

_____

_____

_____

_____

_____

_____

_____

_____

_____

21. My mindful thoughts for the day:

_____

_____

_____

_____

_____

_____

_____

_____

_____

_____

_____

_____

_____

About the authors

Valerie Foster was a journalist, a field rife with constant pressures and deadlines. She has studied many forms of meditation, and a decade ago focused on insight mindfulness meditation, a practice that enters every facet of her daily life – both personal and professional. She wishes she had found this meditation style years ago, but because of mindfulness, doesn't look back and is just so thankful she has it now.

Bill Van Ollefen was as a corporate executive, working all over the globe, until a spinal cord injury caused the worst kind of neurological pain imaginable – the type that often leads to suicide, which he considered often. He turned to insight mindfulness meditation and the effects have been profound. As his practice deepened, his experience with pain evolved. His pain continues to increase, although today it doesn't rule his life, he doesn't suffer, and he is happy, thriving and looking forward to a long life.

They own Pathway to Mindfulness and have helped hundreds of clients live happier, healthier, more focused lives. Both studied Mindfulness-Based Stress Reduction at the University of Massachusetts Medical School, Center for Mindfulness, vipassana meditation at the University of Holistic Theology, and are certified meditation instructors, mindfulness life coaches, cognitive behavioral therapy (CBT) practitioners, CBT life coaches/anxiety specialty and mindfulness CBT practitioners. They are also certified Am I Hungry? teachers.

Loving Kindness Meditation

We start with ourselves
May I be happy
May I be healthy
May I ride the waves of my life
May I live in peace
No matter what I am given

And notice the feelings that arise….

Offer loving kindness to someone
who supports you
May you be happy
May you be healthy
May you ride the waves of your life
May you live in peace
No matter what you are given

And notice the feelings that arise….

Turn your attention now to someone
with whom you have difficulty
May you be happy
May you be healthy
May you ride the waves of your life
May you live in peace
No matter what you are given

And notice the feelings that arise….

And now bring to mind the broader community
May we be happy
May we be healthy
May we ride the waves of our lives
May we live in peace
No matter what we are given

And notice the feelings that arise….

9 781734 722024